IMAGES
of England

HACKNEY
FROM STAMFORD HILL
TO SHOREDITCH

Excited crowds opposite the Town Hall await the arrival of the Prince and Princess of Wales for the official opening of the Hackney Central Library on 28 May 1908. The policemen are keeping a path open to the front of the building to the left of the photographer. Note that the people are all wearing some kind of hat and there is even a postman with his empty sack across his back. The Town Hall was demolished in 1937.

IMAGES
of England

HACKNEY
FROM STAMFORD HILL
TO SHOREDITCH

Compiled by
Gavin Smith

TEMPUS

First published 1999
Copyright © Gavin Smith, 1999

Tempus Publishing Limited
The Mill, Brimscombe Port,
Stroud, Gloucestershire, GL5 2QG

ISBN 0 7524 1818 1

Typesetting and origination by
Tempus Publishing Limited
Printed in Great Britain by
Midway Clark Printing, Wiltshire

The little world of Hackney, 1805. Houses from several centuries line the carriageway, as a two-horse cart rattles through the village. Shop fronts are beginning to dominate the once purely domestic ground floors, while a puny wooden railing protects the shoppers on the footpath. The old church tower sports a mini-steeple.

Contents

Broadway market, London Fields – a very lively market scene in the early years of the twentieth century. The Lord Duncan and the Market House public houses serve the traders and passers by. One of the scores of small boot and shoe makers in the Hackney area – Filmer's – is at No. 26. Apart from working footwear there was a specialist demand from the larger number of folk with foot deformities caused at birth or through accidents, industrial and otherwise, in an age less conscious of health and safety.

Introduction

Hackney was once reputedly part of Stepney (Stebonheath) parish. Already having its own rectory and vicarage by 1292, its church was dedicated to St Augustine. Property in the parish, formerly held by the Order of the Knights Templar, once a very powerful influence in the land, was given on the Templars' suppression to the Knights Hospitaller of St John of Jerusalem. In time the church became known as that of St John in sympathy with the name of the property and manor holdings of the Order. *Leigh's New Picture of London, 1824-5* already describes it as 'an extensive and populous village' and goes on to say 'It is noted as the birth-place of the witty Dr South and the benevolent Howard ... having for its hamlets Upper and Lower Clapton, Shacklewell, Dalston and Homerton. The principal objects worthy of notice are: the mansion at the extremity of Church Street, formerly the residence of John Ward (the South Sea Bubble Swindler) whose infamy has been immortalized by the poet Alexander Pope; the nursery grounds of Messrs Loddiges, containing one of the finest collections of exotic plants in the kingdom; and Brooke House at Clapton. The church, erected in 1797, is a heavy brick building to which a stone steeple and porticoes were added in 1813; the vestibules are ornamented with several monuments brought from the old church, only the tower of which remains. The churchyard is planted with trees, which gives it a very rural appearance, and renders it a pleasant promenade.'

Shoreditch and Hoxton formed the earliest suburbs of the City, in mediaeval times. Later, Nonconformists and others barred from residing within the walls settled here and created a new tolerant community. In the sixteenth century for similar reasons Shoreditch became the focus for a newly fashionable theatre scene of which the authorities were suspicious. Shakespeare came to London and walked the streets of Shoreditch. He acted and wrote for the pioneer Theatre here. He had a financial interest in it and when it relocated to Southwark it was put together with the same materials and in a similar fashion. This means that in the reconstructed Globe Theatre we have a vivid insight into Shoreditch's past. The popularity of The Theatre and its rival The Curtain led to the burial of many theatrical notables in Shoreditch churchyard. Hoxton's fame as a place for alfresco entertainment for Londoners started early. In 1552, Ben Pimlico's nut-brown ale and cakes were celebrated. Pimlico was one of no less than seven ale-houses open for business at this time and Hoxton Street and its environs were a melting pot and meeting place for all classes of people. In the fields behind the street, Ben Jonson killed the actor Gabriel Spencer in a duel in 1598 and narrowly escaped the gallows for it. A portion of Shoreditch extends to the City Road, a new route from Islington and beyond to London built in 1761 across the fields where from time immemorial, archers had practised their skills.

A London County Council tram on route 53, at Manor House en route to Tottenham Court Road via Clapton and Hackney.

One
An Ancient Village
Grows Up

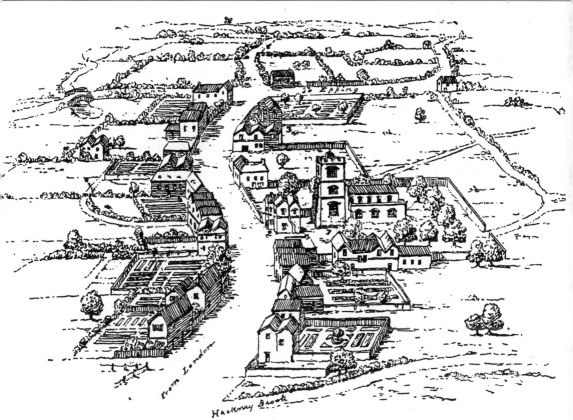

. THE CHURCH OF ST. AUGUSTINE, 1560.   2. THE CHURCH HOUSE.   3. HOUSE AND GROUND
BELONGING TO THE KNIGHTS TEMPLAR BEFORE THE DISSOLUTION OF THEIR ORDER.

A bird's-eye plan of Hackney village, 1560. On the far horizon is the windmill at Stamford Hill.
In the foreground Hackney Brook which ran openly across Mare Street is sketched in.

A milkmaid, a dung cart and haystacks from the fields behind the churchyard in 1776. The

Hackney tower from Homerton – the continuing pastoral scene which in the mid-nineteenth century was about to change to a more urban outlook.

village sat squarely in a rural landscape, and the old buildings on Church Street (as it was then known) stand out against the sky.

A Hackney village view of 1730. The ford through which vehicles had to splash is clearly visible. Pedestrians were able to use the stone bridge on the left or the wooden one on the right. The parish installed lamps on standards to make the crossing less dangerous in the darker hours. The road here as far south as Paragon Road was still known as Church Street although its more recent name of Mare (= mere) Street apparently comes from its watery aspect at this point.

The old church during its demolition in 1799.

By 1840 Church Street was stirring from its slumbers as a quiet village thoroughfare. The number of business premises had grown, and in spite of the flock of sheep in the foreground there was change in the air. In less than ten years construction would begin on the railway with a bridge thrown across the street in the middle distance (beyond the light-fronted houses on the left). The first station opened on the east side of the road but later moved to the west.

A late nineteenth-century photograph of the King's Head public house, not much changed in appearance from the previous illustration. Although this old building remained at this time, a number of other old structures were destroyed by the advent of the railway.

The new church (built in 1797), although the caption describes it as the old. This shows how successfully it had blended into the pattern of the changing town. Standing among the tombs in the extended churchyard, the whole is visible. The thoroughfare from the Homerton direction to Mare Street ensures that it is still part of the centre of town, despite being secluded.

Hackney New Church and the Grammar School echoing some of the church's architectural style. This appears to be the building later called Sutton Lodge which by the beginning of the twentieth century had become a factory.

14

The tower of the former St Augustine's church with the rear of Hackney's first town hall, surviving as a bank building, in the 1920s.

Lower Clapton Road, 1913. At this bend Clapton merges with Hackney. The growth in shopping facilities was as phenomenal as the increase in population that was being served. In 1896 the population was 213,044 – three times that of 1861. However, the town was fortunate to have a number of open spaces remaining.

Looking across from the police station with the northward turn of the Lower Clapton Road in the background behind the new 'General' motor bus on route 22. These shop fronts are extended out from the houses behind on what were once front gardens. The old book and furniture shop next to the tall public baths building in the centre of the picture was still trading into the late 1940s and early '50s.

The new police station of 1904 sits snugly at the back of the churchyard and the beginning of the narrow way into Mare Street, 1910. A shoe-black plies his trade on the opposite kerb – one of the common street scenes of this period.

Watson and Sons' newspaper delivery cart in the early twentieth century. As well as bulk deliveries, the cart would have been used for retail to domestic premises.

The corner of Sutton Place and Urswick Road, 1884. These dignified, tall houses bring to mind the settings of some of Jane Austen's novels.

A view towards the churchyard end of Sutton Place, 1909. The pleasing but mannered architecture is very civilized. This is where Homerton meets Hackney.

Sutton Lodge in 1888. Founded as Hackney Proprietary Grammar School in 1830, it barred the children of local shopkeepers from attending. It later became a residence and in the twentieth century housed part of the Metal Box Company's factory, but was sadly pulled down in the early 1960s.

Towards the bottom end of Mare Street where a turn in the road produces the feature known as 'The Triangle'. It is seen here in 1912 with the electric tram in hot competition with the

recently arrived motor buses. In the middle is the piano factory. At this end of Mare Street the Regent Canal is close and industrial buildings begin to outnumber the shops.

The southern part of Mare Street in 1913. This line of tall tree-shrouded town houses is part of an early nineteenth-century ribbon development. In the distance is the rather elaborate London and Provincial Bank, beyond the church. An impressive trio of early motor buses link Hackney with all other parts of London.

King Edward Road with the bank building of 1897 showing commercial confidence at its height, in 1904.

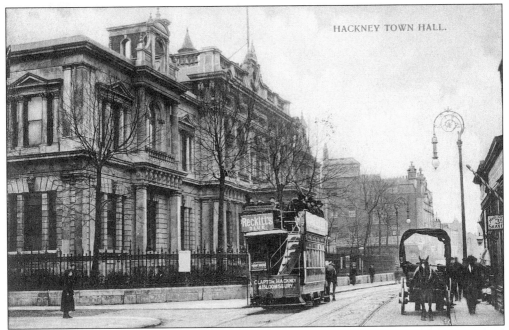

The second Hackney Town Hall rises majestically behind the Clapton, Hackney and Bloomsbury horse-tram, 1903. On the right the buildings flanking the rather narrow main road were demolished for widening and the central library was built behind. Notice the old-style barber's pole and elaborate street lamp on the right.

The narrow section of northern Mare Street. The buildings on the left, seen here in the 1870s, were later demolished as far as Hackney station to widen the roadway. The first Town Hall stood on the site of Church House which had been built in 1520 and taken down in 1802. Only the front of the Town Hall was stone clad at this time. The building housed a manual fire engine and a guardroom for the Parish Watch, a primitive predecessor of the police.

The charming buildings of Lady Holles School, Mare Street, in 1906. In 1930 this was part of the Cripplegate Schools Foundation as a school for girls. Tuition fees were four guineas a term for girls under ten years old and six guineas for those over ten. Various scholarships were available (Foundation Scholarships, Cripplegate Scholarships and Leaving Scholarships) of £30 to £50 per annum.

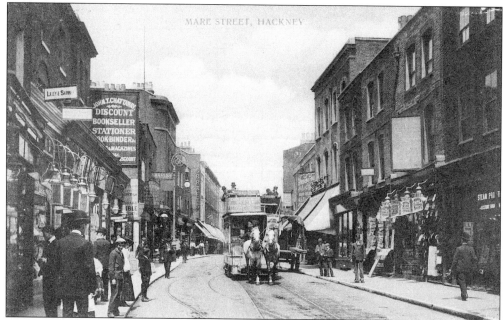

The Tottenham tram in Mare Street, 1904. Edwardian commercial activity directed at the newcomers (among whom are some women for the first time working in offices as typists and file clerks) is really booming. The tram advertises an easy payment system for paying for goods: many would avoid this like the plague, as it was thought to be the quick way to become a debtor and end up in the workhouse or 'union' at Homerton in shameful circumstances.

A policeman keeps a watchful eye at the Graham Road junction with Mare Street in the 1920s. People are boarding the no. 81 tram for Bloomsbury. A large block of lettering on the shop on the left-hand corner invites people to 'furnish as advertised on easy terms'.

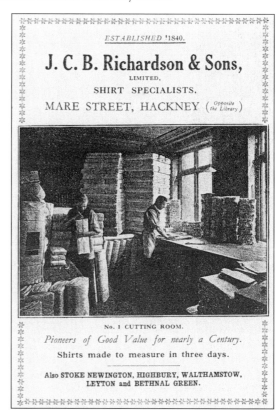

A glimpse of the type of small factory concealed behind the façades of what were once residential buildings, where a multitude of trades did business in 1928.

Barbers Barn, an Elizabethan home located in Mare Street, near the end of Loddyn Road, in 1840. The Countess of Lennox, mother of Lord Darnley, once lived here, surrounded by an estate of splendid gardens.

The Black and White House, Hackney, an ancient building dating from 1578. It is seen here in the 1840s. It stood on the spot where Bohemia Place was built, south of Hackney churchyard. The gateway into it can be seen in the middle of the lower picture on p. 11, behind the Hackney Brook. It had unusually large windows. It was pulled down in 1796.

There is a dramatic tale behind Ward's House which occupied the plot at the corner of Mare Street and Dalston Lane. John Ward, who was responsible for its construction, was the notorious South Sea Bubble swindler. After this view from 1842 it only remained for about five years before being demolished.

The romantically named Navarino Mansions in Dalston Lane were an imaginative venture in the field of housing large numbers of people in one place. They are seen here in 1905 and compare favourably in elegance and design with other large complexes built around London at the end of the Victorian era. Navarino Road, from which they got their name, runs alongside and commemorates the naval battle of that name in 1827 which established Greece's independence as a nation.

A double-fronted villa in Stannard Road illustrates another style of early nineteenth-century Hackney housing suitable for large, reasonably prosperous, middle-class families. At the end of the cul-de-sac can be seen the grandiose entrance and buildings of the German Hospital.

Two

Safe and Well

The concept of looking after the community's health and welfare was one that grew rather slowly. In the Middle Ages strangers in another town or village were liable to be attacked. Only the Church, at first, had some thought for the poor travellers and as most of these were either officials of some sort or pilgrims, very few people left their town or village for any reason in those days. Many people who did undertake the incredibly difficult journeys with all the hazards of attack and exposure to the elements actually died while travelling. The authorities at the time did become interested in setting up lazar or leper hospitals along main roads in order to put away safely people found to be carrying contagious diseases which could often spread like wildfire among populations. The concept of almshouses for aged people grew in Tudor times – rich people would often set up charities for this purpose hoping this would save their souls in the next world. In the nineteenth century and charities and institutions were set up to provide medical care, at an increasing rate. Some were infirmaries to cater for the needs of the destitute in workhouses. Shoreditch and Hoxton had many almshouses, often set up by City companies – a surviving building now houses the Geffrye Museum. Several kinds of hospital were built in the Hackney district in Victorian times including the one at Homerton which was one of those begun as an adjunct to a workhouse (Hackney Union), some distance from the built-up areas. The London Fire Brigade was created in 1804 and was succeeded by increasingly sophisticated fire authorities, which developed throughout the nineteenth century. The old individual fire insurance companies banded together to form the first, known as the London Fire Establishment, in 1833. The Metropolitan Fire Brigade was created in 1865 and had opened twenty-six new fire stations between 1867 and 1871, which revolutionized fire-fighting in the capital.

Certificated nurses at the Homerton Infirmary Hospital attached to the Hackney Union Workhouse, in 1920. The influx of wounded soldiers from the First World War gave a spur to improved medical and training facilities in such institutions.

A primitive-looking motor fire engine of the London Fire Brigade in the 1900s.

The original caption to this picture is somewhat erroneous. The so-called Stoke Newington Fire Station in High Street was neither in Stoke Newington (it was just over the border in Hackney Metropolitan Borough), nor in High Street (rather it was in Leswin Road, a few yards from the High Street). It was built to the usual high standard of these facilities at the time.

Stoke Newington fire fighters line up proudly with their chief fire officer after winning a District Competition for turn-out and fire drill, c. 1912.

Another piece of impressive architecture was the fire station in Kingsland Road. Fire stations today are often placed at the edge of towns to avoid the heavy build-up of traffic on such routes as Kingsland Road. When this view was taken in 1905, traffic although lively caused no serious obstruction to the fire engine's progress.

The large building in the background of the previous picture is here seen close at hand in around 1905. The Metropolitan Hospital was a much-loved centre for medical care up to quite recent times, and it is easy to see how it got its nickname of 'The Grey Lady of Hackney'.

In the children's ward the staffing seems very generous – perhaps this is some kind of celebration, possibly a child's birthday or Christmas. Every effort has been made to make the children as cheerful as the circumstances will allow. Both this and the previous photograph were taken by L.E. Muller of 454 Kingsland Road.

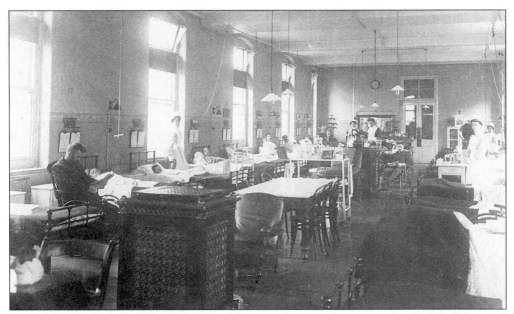

A men's ward at the Metropolitan. There is a good ratio of nurses to patients and the ward appears well equipped. A patent heating system of the type once very familiar in public institutions appears in the foreground. The young age of many of the patients and the presence of some wheelchairs suggest a date after the First World War had started in 1914, when the hospital was receiving wounded soldiers.

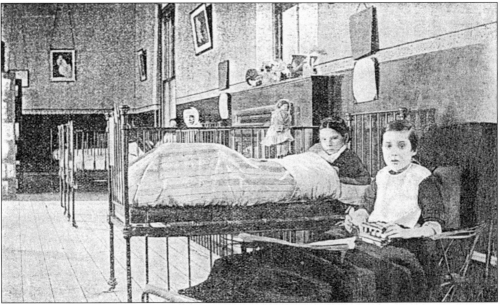

This earlier picture of children in cots at the Metropolitan apparently on a bare board floor reminds us that these hospitals were set up by the efforts of pioneers such as the Quaker families of Fry, Gurney and Hoare to provide facilities for the care of the poor when ill. After the actual buildings were set up there was often a continual struggle to raise money for the running of the hospital and the provision of facilities. New benefactors had constantly to be sought through special appeals and sometimes funds were short for furnishing the wards.

A photograph of the extensive buildings connected with the pioneering German Hospital, off Dalston Lane, probably in the late 1920s.

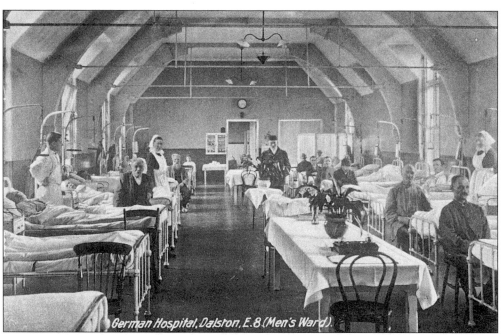

A men's ward at the hospital, with visitors. Most of the Germans in London were men and they tended to work in the East End in some of the less healthy trades such as sugar boiling and skin drying and dressing. Partly because of their different language and culture they had difficulty in being recommended for hospital treatment by letter from the appropriate person, which was the usual way of getting into a voluntary hospital at the time.

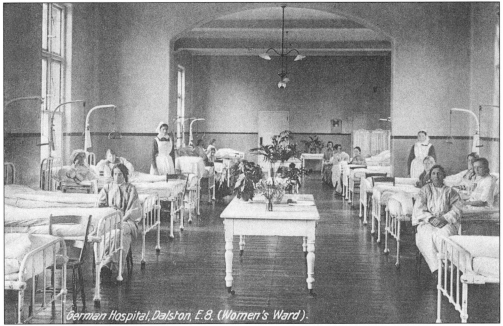

A light and airy women's ward. From its foundation and opening in the 1840s, when it took over the former infant orphan asylum estate at Hackney in order to provide care for the sick Germans in London, it was both successful in attracting good sources of financing and in remaining in the lead with new medical advances. Germans were the largest immigrant group in London in the nineteenth century, far outnumbering all other nationalities.

Another view from the German Hospital in the 1920s shows a waiting crowd of women wondering how long it will be before they get to see a doctor. A porter is ready, while nurses and doctors have come out to see the photograph taken. The facilities were also available to non-Germans.

This sweeping view of the shut-off enclave occupied by this unique hospital was probably taken from the railway embankment in the 1930s and shows, from left to right, the modern Burnet, Tait and Lorne Extension, the earlier ranges including the main entrance up steps to the Donaldson building and the Hamburg Lutheran church by the Ritson Road gates.

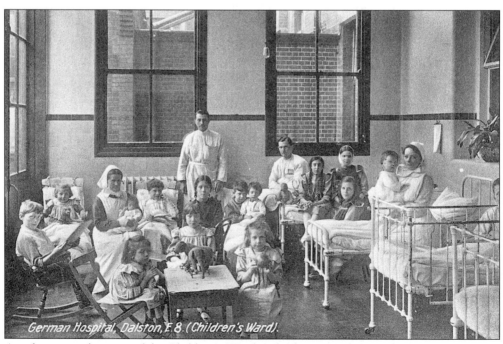

Another view, this time of the Children's Ward with play activities.

Hackney citizens, as those elsewhere, were becoming more aware of health issues in the 1920s and 1930s. Many local authorities were providing clinics, including post-natal mother and baby care. In addition, as this advertisement shows, there were agencies providing private nurses on demand for particular kinds of nursing in the home.

Do you want me ?

Then please 'Phone
CLISSOLD 3039.

My Matron (Mrs. Benjafield) supplies Trained Nurses, Midwives, Fever Nurses and Assistant Nurses.

Special Terms for Institutions.

Highfield Nurses' Institute

MRS. BENJAFIELD, LTD.
──── (Estd. 1908) ────
4, Amhurst Park, Stamford Hill, N. 16.

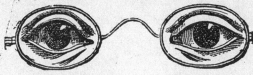

OPHTHALMIC OPTICIAN.
Established 100 Years.
All persons suffering from
DEFECTIVE VISION,
should consult MR. LAMBE, the only Ophthalmic Optician in Stoke Newington.

The Sight tested daily by competent Opticians, and suitable **Spectacles** supplied from **1s. per pair.**

MR. LAMBE,
211, High Street
STOKE NEWINGTON.
Four Doors from Abney Park Cemetery.

Gold and Steel Spectacle Maker.

All Kinds of Repairs done on the Premises
[282]

Another growth area was that of opticians. E.G. Lambe of 211 High Street, Stoke Newington was only one of the numerous premises devoted to eye care.

The Queen's Hospital for Children in Hackney Road was officially in Bethnal Green but it was always thought of as a Shoreditch location, the Borough boundary running down the side and round the back of the building. It was still giving wonderful treatment to East London's many young people until very recently when it was closed.

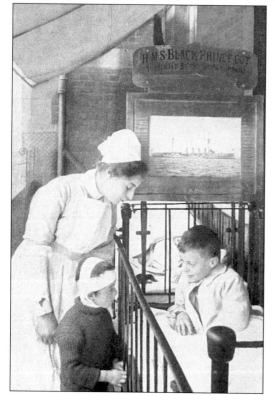

A fundraising postcard of the cot supported by the Ships Company of HMS *Black Prince*, after the ship's sinking. It seems that the wonderful system of sponsorship that had been built up extended to nearly every bed provided.

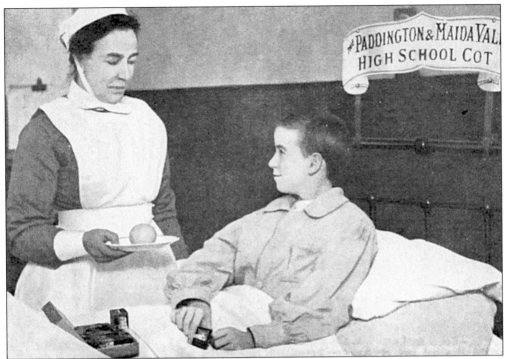

Queen Alexandra remained as Patron of the hospital after the death of her husband Edward VII. This bed is provided by the girls of the Paddington and Maida Vale High School who made sacrifices in order to provide funds for it. Is it an apple that Sister is bringing the young patient?

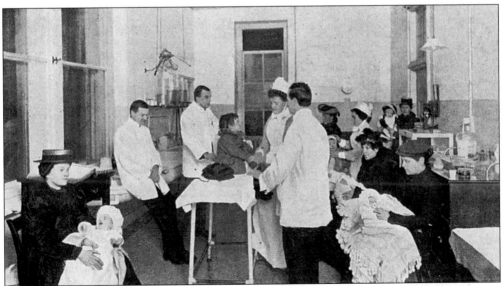

The new casualty room at the Queen's Hospital in the early years of the century, before royal patronage when it was still known as the North Eastern Hospital for Children. It later became Queen Elizabeth's Hospital after the old Queen's death. Its 114 beds at this time were always full, showing the tremendous need that existed in the East End for children's medical facilities.

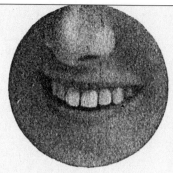

A vivid illustration for false teeth by Messrs Thomas & Co. of 362 Mare Street (the narrow part), c. 1908. Around this time there were many advertisements connected with tooth care in books, journals and newspapers. Mr F.E. Ford of 100 Mare Street and York House, Brookfield Road, South Hackney, also advertised 'High-class Artificial Teeth', pointing out the digestive problems caused by missing molars. The Clapton Teeth Institute of Clapton Passage claimed that they were experts in every branch of dentistry and, more improbably, that they had never had a dissatisfied patient! W. Sharman of 186 Mare Street advertised 'Prize Medal Artificial Teeth', with a price list including a single tooth for 3s 6d and a complete set for a guinea. Finally, Thomas Jones, a jeweller of 385 Mare Street, offered cash for artificial teeth and old gold and silver.

Three
Stamford Hill and Upper Clapton

Roman Ermine Street climbed this hill and the wild country round about would have made quite an impression on the travellers of that time. The view from the top was impressive as late as the nineteenth century. It was along this way that the Scottish King James VI, now to become James I of England, came on his last leg to London, which must have been visible on the horizon from its many church towers and smoking chimneys. On 7 May 1603 an observer described the scene as the new King descended the hill: 'The multitudes of people in high wayes, fieldes, medowes, closes and on trees were such, that they covered the beautie of the fieldes, and so greedy were they to behold the countenance of the King, that with much unruliness they injured and hurt one another, some even hazarded to the daunger of death...all the way as his Majestie past with shoutes and cries, and casting up of hattes...'

It has been suggested that the name Stamford comes from there having been at the bottom of the hill by Abney Park Cemetery a 'stony ford' over the Hackney Brook which crossed here. The Ambulator Guide to London and its Environs (11th edition, 1811) says of Stamford Hill: 'The upper part of Clapton...containing many well-built houses raised on an eminence, which command a pleasing prospect of the adjacent county.' This entry was probably originally written in the late eighteenth century showing that the later residential suburb had an early start.

Achievement in Life: 35 Portland Avenue, Stamford Hill. People were so proud to live in a good residential area that they sent out postcard views of their homes as Christmas cards and invitations. In this case the respectability is particularly high: there are net curtains at all the windows, window boxes and front railings.

LOT 9.

The Attractively Built

LONG LEASEHOLD

CORNER VILLA RESIDENCE

BEING

No. 36, Fairview Road,

STAMFORD HILL, N.

Situate within a few minutes' walk of Stamford Hill (Gt. Eastern) and South Tottenham (Midland) Railway Stations, and close to the Main Road with Motor 'Bus and Electric Tram Services.

The House is constructed in Red and Stock Brick with Double Bays, Stone Dressings and Tiled Roof. It is approached through a neat Front Garden enclosed by Dwarf Wall and Wooden Palings, and the accommodation comprises:

ON THE UPPER FLOOR.—Two Front Bedrooms, one with Embayed Window, Ornamental Mantel, Slow Combustion Stove with Tiled Sides and Hearth and a Cupboard. A Back Bedroom fitted with Ornamental Mantel, Stove and Cupboard. Bathroom with Bath and Lavatory Basin (h. and c. supplies). Linen Cupboard. Separate W.C.

ON THE LOWER FLOOR.—Front Reception Room with Embayed Window Ornamental Mantel, Slow Combustion Stove with Tiled Sides and Hearth. Back Room fitted with Range, Glazed Dresser, and Casement Door opening into Garden. Scullery with Tiled Floor, Sink (h. and c. supplies), and Copper. Larder, Cupboard under, Stairs. W.C.

Pleasant Garden in Rear with separate Side Entrance.   **Modern Drainage.**

Let to Mr. WM. GINGER on a yearly tenancy at the Low Rent of **16/-** per week, or equivalent to

Per £41 12s. Ann.

THE LANDLORD PAYING RATES AND TAXES.

Held on Lease for 99 years from the 29th day of September, 1905 (leaving over 85 years unexpired) at a Ground Rent of £5 10s. per annum.

Part of an auction leaflet for leasehold residence ground rents. There are three villas involved in Fairview Road – nos 36, 38 and 46 – together producing £124 16s, which would have made a comfortable retirement income at the time (1919). The details give a good insight into the kind of accommodation provided by a typical house on Stamford Hill.

Stamford Hill Mansions in 1904. These apartments were frequently lived in by emigrés from continental Europe, where apartments were more the norm, even in those days.

The North Hackney Constitutional Club took over one of the oldest mansions from the early period of the Hill's development in the early 1900s. Previously it had been occupied by Thomas Windus FSA and was known as Gothic Hall because of an annexe built in Gothic style which was open to the roof timbers inside and intended as a museum.

Stamford Hill originally had space to house many institutions, among them St Mary's Priory, seen here, with extensive gardens for rest and meditation.

A classroom in the Priory, c. 1920. There is an interesting combination of domestic and academic furniture.

Northfield Road – a representative street view on Stamford Hill in 1903. With little traffic passing through and no parked cars or other vehicles, the roadway seems generously wide.

The Stamford Hill horse-bus. There was something noble about travelling to a superior City workplace from a desirable Stamford Hill residence behind two black horses, your course straight as an arrow down the old Ermine Street with only an occasional swerve to avoid some other vehicle.

St Ignatius' church towers above the lower slopes in 1913.

Stamford Hill was an early location for training establishments of all kinds. Here, around 1903, is the spacious Physical Laboratory of St Ignatius' College.

Going to the shops above St Ignatius' church in 1912. Tram wires criss-cross the street as a heavy motor vehicle toils up the hill behind a horse carriage with large wheels.

Tram Terminus, Stamford Hill.

Wright's Photo Series
Stamford Hill

In 1916 Sainsbury's have gained a prime location in the fairly new main shopping area by the Stamford Hill tram terminus.

Open for business by Stoke Newington Station entrance. All the shops at the bottom of
Stamford Hill have their blinds in use to keep the sun off their goods. They include a fruiterer,
a dairy, a draper, a furniture dealer, a milliner, a ladies' outfitter, a drug store, a confectioner, a
tobacconist, a stationer, a tea store and a sub-post office. There were no empty shops and no
supermarkets. This is the Jazz Age of the 1920s and a hoarding above the station advertises the

delights of a new film at the Coliseum Cinema. Although motor car ownership is confined to the few, another advertisement recommends 'buy your car from R. Garwood'. This large motor agency had a number of premises in the local area including three on Stamford Hill. Above the station Fisher Stanhope, auctioneers, are well placed to intercept travellers coming by rail in search of a local property to buy or rent.

In 1902 horse-buses, a tram and some people congregate near the Bird Cage public house, a Truman Hanbury and Buxton supplied premises. On the horse bus in the side road a Brock's Firework display at the Crystal Palace is advertised.

On the corner of Rookwood Road and Clapton Common an impressive church with a tall spire and carved winged beasts representing the four evangelists housed the Agapemonite Sect. The founder H.J. Prince died in 1899 shortly after the completion of the building in 1896. In 1902 his successor John Hugh Smyth-Pigott was installed and proclaimed himself the Messiah. This shocked the locals who were liable to heckle and chase him. This satirical postcard shows scenes from the evolving scandal with Smyth-Pigott in the middle holding the results of his tenet of free love. He somehow attracted legions of women followers who are shown besieging the church and worshipping at his feet. He and his followers eventually fled to Somerset.

50

Cazenove Road in 1902, at this time a delightful tree-lined boulevard in miniature. The placing of the lighting standard in the middle of the roadway shows just how much times have changed.

Part of Upper Clapton Road at the same date. The Upper Clapton Dairy is down the alley at the left – premises later taken over, like many others, by United Dairies Ltd. Beyond the two houses is the Congregational church and a grocer's shop.

Having completed his round on Clapton Common, a postman stands to attention for the camera in front of the interesting architecture of St Thomas's church, 1904.

A large crowd of supporters and onlookers fill Stamford Hill in a religious procession involving the Master of the Guild of Ransom with the Ransom Crucifix and Acolytes presumably from St Ignatius' church nearby. The photographer is Reinhold Thiele, the date around 1910.

A gentleman in a top hat pauses on the pavement as a horse tram and lady cyclist approach along the Common in 1903. A constable takes note and almost appears to be reaching for his notebook. The authorities probably kept an eye on the wide open spaces of the greensward which might be a suitable spot for nefarious activities, such as preparations for burglary in the well furnished villas behind.

A closer view of the residences at the back of Clapton Common. Those in view are quite recent properties with an art nouveau dwarf fence. A tiny dairy float of the old kind stands at the kerb in 1913.

A vista past the playing fields and cricket ground in Spring Hill which leads down to the bridge over the Lea and the marshes, 1905. At the bottom, in the nineteenth century, there was a tile-making business with its own dock on the river.

Springfield Park, 1904. This open space was created for the people by various benefactors, some of whom gave up their own houses to make it larger and to provide wonderful views over the Lea and marshes to Coppermill. It was a particular haven for local children.

Four

Clapton

In the sixteenth century Brooke House, opposite the corner of Lea Bridge and Lower Clapton Roads, was the property of Henry Algernon Percy, sixth Earl of Northumberland, who lived here and was buried in old Hackney church. The house was occupied by a succession of famous residents, including Queen Margaret of Scotand, Elizabeth, Queen of Edward IV, Sir William Herbert, Earl of Pembroke and Margaret, Lady Lennox (James I's grandmother). The name came from the famous Fulke Greville (the first Lord Brooke). Another important possessor was Edward de Vere, Earl of Oxford, one of the claimants to authorship of Shakespeare's plays. Pepys and Evelyn both mention the house and its gardens in their diaries. Pepys recorded in a visit in 1666, how he first saw oranges growing '…some green, some a quarter and some full ripe on the same tree…. I pulled off a little one by stealth and ate it'. In 1920 the house was used as a private mental asylum. Unfortunately this mansion was heavily damaged in an air raid on the night of 8 September 1940 and in spite of running repairs it had to be demolished in 1954. A monograph by the London County Council fully describes its history and architecture. *Kelly's Directory* of 1874 describes Clapton – '…a hamlet and ecclesiastical parish formed in 1863 out of Hackney civil parish … about a mile from Lea Bridge station on the Great Eastern Railway…. St James' church is Gothic in the Early English style; the reredos is remarkable for its beauty…. There are four schools in connection with this church (showing the growth in population in the nineteenth century, Bishop Wood's Almshouses and a Grammar School in connection with King's College, London…. Near the Lea Bridge station is a large india-rubber manufactory. The population in 1871 was 3,953.'

A charming riverside scene on the River Lea, *c.* 1906. This little community had grown up naturally over the years with the Beehive and Robin Hood pubs, cottages small factories and boatyards.

A 'rustic' old bridge adds romance to Clapton Pond Gardens, *c.* 1904. Back gardens were filled with benches, tables and other features in this style which had been made popular in the late nineteenth century. Large stores such as Gamages and Harrods included dozens of types in their thick catalogues.

56

The cold-drink seller at work on the far bank of the Lea which is gaily decorated. From this point there is a good view of the holiday activities on the Clapton Bank.

A moonlit view of the birthplace of John Howard, the prison reformer, at Clapton in the 1840s. At this stage the area was still quite rural.

JOHN HOWARD Efq.ʳ F.R.S.

Taken from Nature. March 1788.

Howard threw himself into the study of prison conditions without sparing himself. He is remembered today in the name of the Howard League for Penal Reform.

'Seek Ye The Lord'. The Waterloo Rooms in 1932 were believed to be one of the oldest buildings in Hackney Borough. Standing in Prout Road, Clapton, the building's early history was shrouded in mystery. It had been a religious building for a long time, first as a meeting place for the Plymouth Brethren, where Edmund Gosse, the famous essayist worshipped as a child, and later as Mission Rooms.

Chatsworth Road Market and shopping area – a very typical Edwardian venue for all local shopping needs. There was a good range of stores, including a fish and chip shop, shoemaker,

ironmonger, baker, general grocer, chemist, hosier, tobacconist, dairy, fishmonger, hairdresser and even an undertaker.

The family and staff of a butcher's shop in Chatsworth Road line up outside in front of the usual display of hanging meat – a practice which would be thought unhygienic today. By 1930 the shop was still a pork butchers but had passed from the Beyers to Curtis & Son.

The interchange between tram and train at Clapton station. In the 1870s this line was still under construction and travellers had to make for Lea Bridge or Hackney stations to make the rail link into the City.

The Howard County Secondary School, Clapton, in the 1930s. It was renamed after John Howard, the prison reformer. It was a progressive school, built with modern facilities when contrasted with the large multi-storey Victorian temples of learning.

The multi-purpose hall of the Howard School was designed to admit more light than the older inner-London school buildings and the stage itself could be used as a teaching area.

The corner of Lea Bridge Road and Lower Clapton Road is now a traffic-choked junction and it is surprising to see this peaceful, friendly scene from around 1906 with fishmongers, butchers, tobacconists and grocers prominent.

A group of seventeen boys, sporting cloth caps, watch the photographer at work in about 1913 on the leafy side of Tresham Avenue. It seems to be a holiday and they are perhaps waiting to go on a Sunday school outing. Ina few short years some will go to fight in the First World War and be killed in France – part of the lost generation.

The Salvation Army has been a strong force for social improvement and care in Hackney and these attractive nineteenth-century homes in Clapton, seen in around 1915, house a typical venture – the Mothers' Hospital.

Osbaldeston Road, Clapton, with its gentle curve, illustrates a particular type of respectable residential area in 1903. Trees were always being planted in such roads to try to create a more rural effect.

The Grocers' Company School – on of the many City foundations that had moved their institutions from the crowded City into the suburbs where more of the young families were living in the late nineteenth century. The impressive building with an open outlook is seen here in 1903.

Part of the open aspect of Hackney Downs, with a drinking fountain as its focal point. In a less sophisticated age drinking fountains supplied a much needed source of clean water for travellers and children playing in the park.

Five

The Old Road

Once the main route to Lincoln and York, the Roman Ermine Street runs southwards from the bottom of Stamford Hill where the Hackney Brook used to cross the road close to the Abney Park Cemetery. Just off the High Road between 1878 and 1883 an archaeologist named Worthington Smith uncovered implements from the Old Stone Age. Excavations on the south side of Stoke Newington Common revealed 'an immense accumulation' of flint tools that had been abandoned for some reason by the earliest inhabitants. Later, when Alkham, Kyverdale, Osbaldeston and Fountayne Roads were begun, hundreds of flint implements were recovered. Another researcher, J.E. Greenhill, said of the finds: 'all these implements and flakes found at a particular level were quite unabraded … presenting the appearance of having just left the hand of the workman'. Other finds were made all along the route of the old road at Stamford Hill, Kingsland and Shacklewell, showing how far back this area was inhabited, perhaps even before the wild forest of Middlesex had taken root here. As our modern road goes south it successively becomes Stoke Newington High Street, Stoke Newington Road and Kingsland Road – for the greater part the shops have been almost continuous during the twentieth century, part of the great consumer boom. Only public houses and official buildings interrupt the progress as far as Kingsland Gate or Dalston. A number of theatres and from the 1920s cinemas also intervened. South of Dalston to the Canal, there lies Kingsland Waste or Plain, an area at the east side of the road where an informal market is held and in Edwardian times preachers did their best to spread the word of the Lord. By the canal, wharves and factories and many industrial trades flourished but since the Second World War these have declined and have slowly been replaced by newer enterprises. In this picture of Kingsland High Street, nearly opposite Ridley Road Market in around 1910, is the closed Dalston Kingsland station, just beyond Warbey's and Lea's shops. The station has now reopened on this site.

Abney Park Cemetery at the top end of the High Road contains Dr Watt's monument. He lived at one time in Abney House, which once occupied the site of the cemetery, and his effigy now looks out over the tombs of fellow Nonconformists who flourished in this area as a self-contained community after being driven out of the City in earlier centuries.

An advertisement for E.G. Lambe's opticians shop from an Edwardian directory. This shop begins several miles of shopping facilities, stretching almost unbroken to Dalston.

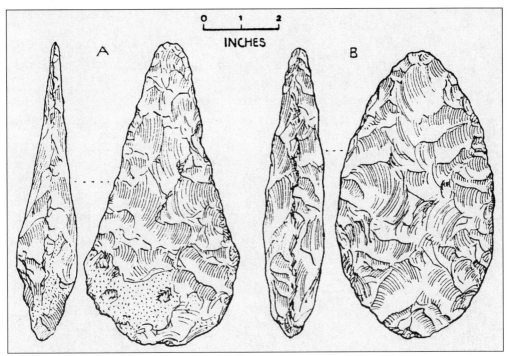

Flint implements of the kind found in their hundreds in Alkham, Kyverdale and other roads.

Built in 1712, this delightful house at 187 High Street is still in use today, having had many roles during its long existence. Here in 1906 it is the Invalid Asylum. Later, in the 1930s, it was the Home Hospital for Women. It continues to give Stoke Newington real character, something sadly lacking in other places in an age of monolithic standardization.

Stoke Newington High Street by West Hackney church in 1907. The smart electric trams ran the length of the road from Stamford Hill to Shoreditch church. Maynard's the confectioners and sweet makers have an office and premises here on the corner of Gordon Road.

Kingsland High Street, Dalston, sometimes known as Kingsland Gate, was always a focal point with busy shopping facilities. As well as being the site of Dalston Junction station, this was a crossing point and interchange for buses going north and south along the road with others going east and west to Hackney or Islington and points beyond. This is a 1905 view looking north to Stoke Newington.

Amhurst Road – which runs from West Hackney church to the centre of Hackney by Hackney station – was probably built on the line of an old footpath across the fields. By the early twentieth century it had become a major thoroughfare. It was mainly residential, but had a few shops and churches along its length as well.

Another view of Kingsland Gate with competing horse bus and tram in 1904. Behind the bus is the entrance to Dalston Lane with the Crown and Castle pub.

71

The little-known Dalston Manor House in the late nineteenth century. It stood inside its grounds on the north side of Dalston Lane, to the east of a more modern house known as Graham House. There was a beautiful plantation of trees behind it. It was demolished in 1923/24 and some flats, the Lewis Trust Dwellings, were built on the site.

This part of Dalston Lane, containing the German Hospital entrance, has a certain continental feel about in this view from 1904. Many of the nurses and patients still wore a costume from their own country adding an exotic touch to the neighbourhood.

On this bend in Dalston Lane in 1904 are the Three Compasses pub, the Swanton Farm Dairy and a barbers and hairdressers. The route taken by this road follows the path of a very ancient green lane.

A typical Victorian suburban road in Dalston built in terraces with later shop development at the end: this is Norfolk Road in 1908.

St Columba's church, Kingsland Road, 1903. This was a massive piece of architecture, again with signs of Continental influence, but constructed without thought of the ongoing costs of maintenance. It was, however, a much-loved centre of community activities.

The Potter Brothers' Steam Printing Works at 440-442 Kingsland Road faced earlier Victorian villa terraces on the south side, breaking the almost continuous line of shops from Stoke Newington. In 1900, Potters was still the location of the *Hackney and Kingsland Gazette* office. There is an informal market along this wide stretch of the roadside known as Kingsland Plain or Kingsland Waste. Various religions also used this area for preaching the word of God to passers-by.

Part of Kingsland Road dominated by the Metropolitan Hospital. An elegant street lamp helps to disperse the gloom of fog or smoke as the road approaches the industrial and wharf region near the Regent's Canal to the south.

The newly erected shed and timber wharf put up by the firm of J. Kennedy & Co. on Union Wharf West, Kingsland Road, in the 1920s. The Regent's Canal provides a way of transporting heavy materials alongside.

Six

The Tide of Commerce

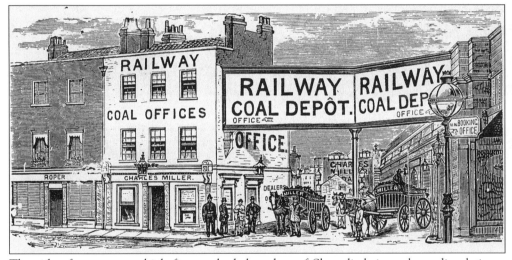

The tide of commerce which first washed the edges of Shoreditch in early medieval times, having flowed from the City, had by the early twentieth century grown into a sea as far as Hackney and its area was concerned. The early ribbon development along Bishopsgate outside the City gate reached Shoreditch High Street via Norton Folgate in a continuous line northwards. It may even have had its origin in Roman times with booths providing services to those embarking on a journey along Ermine Street or Old Street. Certainly we can envisage medieval merchants having a foothold here above their places of work which may not have yet received the seal of approval of the City Guilds. Hostels may have provided shelter for those who reached the City gate too late to beat the curfew – they then had to find a night's lodging outside the gate but preferably away from the hazards of the open street, fields and marshes beyond. The houses which lined these streets had nearly all become commercial premises in part or whole by the nineteenth century. Further out in the villages of Hackney, Clapton and Homerton there were still dairies and farms as well as incipient industries, mills and factories, by the River Lea or in other convenient locations. Later canals and wharves brought in large quantities of raw materials, such as timber for the furniture industry which was prominent in the Shoreditch area, and heavy metal items for engineering works. Charles Miller's coal depot, next to Hackney station in the nineteenth century. Coal was the most important fuel for home and industry into the twentieth century and this firm were suppliers for over 100 years.

Although large tonnages of coal were transported by railway, many goods and raw materials came along canals and rivers like the Lea. Many industries were sited along the Lower Lea in South Hackney, Homerton and by Hackney Marshes close to its junction with the river Thames.

One of Hackney's countless factories, Berry's produced various kinds of polishes.

H. Moreau at their Cazenove Works were very proud of their 30-yard automatic embroidery machine. This is a view of the factory and machine around 1912.

D. Politi's trade card. A number of confectionery factories were located in the Hackney area.

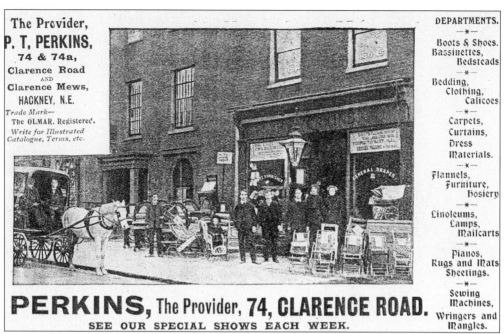

The Provider,
P. T. PERKINS,
74 & 74a,
Clarence Road
AND
Clarence Mews,
HACKNEY, N.E.

Trade Mark—
The OLMAR, Registered.
Write for Illustrated
Catalogue, Terms, etc.

DEPARTMENTS.
— ✻ —
Boots & Shoes.
Bassinettes,
Bedsteads
— ✻ —
Bedding,
Clothing,
Calicoes
— ✻ —
Carpets,
Curtains,
Dress
Materials.
— ✻ —
Flannels,
Furniture,
Hosiery
— ✻ —
Linoleums,
Lamps,
Mailcarts
— ✻ —
Pianos,
Rugs and Mats
Sheetings.
— ✻ —
Sewing
Machines,
Wringers and
Mangles.

PERKINS, The Provider, **74, CLARENCE ROAD.**
SEE OUR SPECIAL SHOWS EACH WEEK.

P.T. Perkins tried to take a leaf out of the big London stores' books – they were known as Universal Providers to encompass, in a phrase, their wide range of stock.

In 1905 one of the fastest-growing retail stores, which had taken over four shops at nos 121-127 Kingsland Road, sent out this postcard to their known customers and others with a handwritten message: 'Our great Summer Sale commences Friday July 14. Enquire for Catalogue.'

A view by the shops in Maury Road which ran between Northwold and Kenninghall Road in 1907. Although according to the Post Office this was part of Stoke Newington, it was actually within Hackney Metropolitan Borough. This view at the Stoke Newington Common end shows on the left the entrance to the laundry run by the Salvation Army. Many people boiled some of their clothes in gas-fired coppers at home, while laundries supplied a large white linen bag to fill with dirty washing which they would launder for a standard charge. This was common until the advent of modern washing machines in the 1960s.

One of the more progressive shoe shops among the great number to be found in Hackney, c. 1909. This is at 128 Well Street, South Hackney. Boots were often made as well as repaired and sold inside these shops. Stout footwear was important when many working-class people walked for miles to save money on transport.

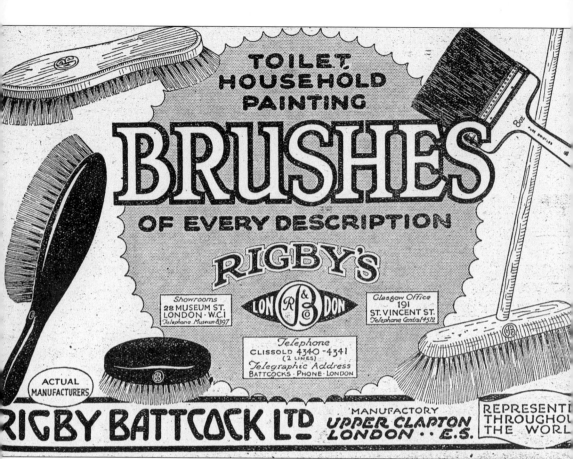

This Clapton brush-making factory advertised its products in the 1929 Buff Book or *Trade and Commercial Directory for London.*

An old trade located in Homerton advertises what it can do in 1908.

N. MARDALL,

Coach, Van & Cart Builder,

96, High Street, HOMERTON, N.E.

When wanting any Repairs to Vehicles ring up

1845 DALSTON.

MOTOR BODIES BUILT TO ANY DESIGN.

Vehicles Built, Supplied, and Repaired by Contract.

ESTIMATES & DRAWINGS SUBMITTED FREE.

TYRING DAILY.

The celebration of the 1935 Silver Jubilee of King George V's reign gave the Gas Light & Coke Company an opportunity to light up their premises in a spectacular fashion.

83

The purchase of a piano was the aspiration of a great number of people from the start of the century, although only an upright model would fit into most homes, not the grand version featured on Parker's publicity.

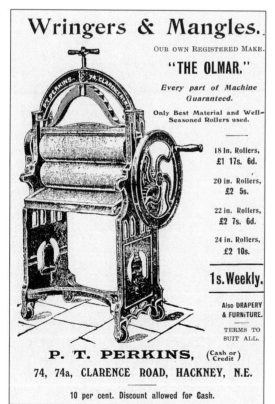

The mangle offered by P.T. Perkins was a feature of most homes earlier in the twentieth century, used to squeeze the water out of clothes and other washing straight from the copper or washbowl.

The Stoke Newington premises of Pocock's Dairies in Leswin Road, *c.* 1913. This and the Lower Clapton address were by the 1930s taken over by the United Dairies combine.

Pocock's Dairies

B. POCOCK & SONS, Proprietors.

DAIRIES:

Leswin Road, - Stoke Newington, N.
103, Upper Clapton Road, Clapton, N.
107, Lower Clapton Road, Clapton, N.E.

Genuine Rich New Milk, clean and well-cooled, delivered throughout the surrounding districts, also in the districts of Finsbury Park, Mildmay Park and Newington Green.

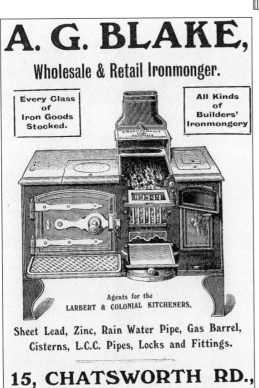

A. G. BLAKE,

Wholesale & Retail Ironmonger.

Every Class of Iron Goods Stocked.

All Kinds of Builders' Ironmongery

Agents for the
LARBERT & COLONIAL KITCHENERS.

Sheet Lead, Zinc, Rain Water Pipe, Gas Barrel, Cisterns, L.C.C. Pipes, Locks and Fittings.

15, CHATSWORTH RD.,
Clapton Park, N.E.

Ironmongers sold these solid fuel kitchen cookers at the beginning of the century. Gas cooking was available but good electric cookers took some time to develop.

This house premises is being used as a second hand goods shop, *c*. 1910. Notice the cages above the front door containing singing birds which were popularly bought and sold at this period.

Seven

Homerton and South Hackney

These districts lie on the east and south of Hackney, bordering Hackney Marsh, the Lea and the Regent's Canal and Victoria Park. Homerton takes its name from 'Hunburh's farm or holding'. It became part of the manor of Lordshold which was held successively by the Knights Templar and, when their influence waned, by the Knights of St John of Jerusalem, two immensely powerful forces in the land. The Templars had established at least one mill complex on the Lea (still known as Temple Mills) and possibly more, creating a prosperous economy in this area. A community slowly developed and created a meeting place. The numerous raised pavements alongside the important Homerton streets were designed to protect the pedestrian from the all-pervasive mud, churned up by early traffic. A famous son of the seventeenth century, Sir Thomas Sutton, Paymaster of the Northern Army and Victualler of the Navy, occupied Sutton House on the High Street, very close to Hackney churchyard and village. In the mid-nineteenth century, in spite of the increasing number of factories to the south and the development of an estate in the middle of Homerton by Lewis Berger, the paint, colour and varnish manufacturer, there were still watercress beds near where Chalgrove Road was built. However, their demise was hastened by the construction of the railway viaduct across the area. J. Hews spares a few minutes from his long working day to be photographed at the door of his boot-making premises.

What They Did In The Great War.

L. E. Cornell, R.E., wounded Gallipoli, awarded M.M.
Cyril W. Cornell, London Regt., killed.
Sec.-Lt. A. G. Cornell, killed.

The three sons of Mr. C. Cornell, of South Hackney.

This South Hackney family's sons paid a high price for fighting in the First World War.

A South Hackney secondary school room in around 1910 doubles as the School Library, although the book stock seems rather limited and is carefully stowed away in bookcases – perhaps for use by only the brighter scholars. Some school desks of the type shown here survived into the 1940s.

A glimpse of the area around St John's church, South Hackney.

The Regent's Canal skirts the south end of Hackney and passes through part of the old Shoreditch Borough before reaching a semi-rural section at the bottom end of Victoria Park. This park has been a welcome open space for the people of Homerton and South Hackney since its opening in 1845.

The Higher Grade School in Cassland Road, South Hackney, had an unusual and interesting exterior design, seen here in 1903.

An important South Hackney shopping area at Lauriston Road on a horse-tram route.

An amazing episode took place on Hackney Marshes in 1911. Soldiers camped out there as an emergency measure during that year's rail strike.

The local photographer T.S. Robinson records a party, probably from the local church, at the start of a day's outing by charabanc in the 1920s. The party mostly consists of ladies who have dressed to look their best while catering for changes in the weather. The holiday atmosphere in the foreground makes an interesting contrast with the smoking chimneys and grey streets of industrial Homerton seen in the background.

An old house near the railway arch in Bridge Street, Homerton. A stone tablet on the front, seen here in the 1930s, contained an illustration of a pair of scales and the wording: 'This is Bridge Street. Homerton. Houndsrow.' It may have been once used as a magistrates' court as fireplaces in the house were said to have had the Royal Coat of Arms worked on them at a previous date.

Homerton chapel in an old engraving. This is said to be the oldest proprietary chapel in the kingdom; Stephen Ram, a Lombard Street banker, founded it in 1829.

Ram's Chapel was renovated in 1910 and continued to serve a religious function in the 1930s among some very poor housing. A beautiful pulpit inside was the work of Grinling Gibbons and there were some stained glass windows of quality.

Morning Lane as it appeared in the 1850s. Many of the ancient houses had disappeared by the beginning of the twentieth century but in the late 1920s some primitive dwellings survived in the area beyond Stockmar Road. On Rocque's Plan of 1745 this lane is represented as Money Lane and at other times as Mourning and Moor Hen Lane. Nearby were the famous Homerton watercress beds fed by water diverted from the Hackney Brook which disappeared shortly after this time.

Homerton fire station, one of the newer buildings in the village, *c.* 1908.

Church Road, showing some of the typical raised pavements protecting pedestrians and dating back to earlier times. Note the sign on the undertaker's premises centre left: 'Respectable Funerals'. The message on the back of this 1904 card refers to Homerton as 'the little old smoky village'.

One of the private fire brigades run by the bigger factories is seen here in a very military turnout in 1923, after winning two awards (the London Private Fire Brigade Association's Nestle Cup and the National Fire Brigade Association's Hose Cart Cup).

Two Homerton families and their trades. Henry Arthur Smith and his wife lived at 29 Hassett Road, Homerton in the 1930s and '40s. Henry had come down to the East End as a young man to ply his trade as a journeyman cooper in the London Docks and breweries. Wooden barrels were used to store and transport not only beer but a great number of other cargoes. Henry was born in Burton in 1867 and first lived in the Limehouse area of London. In 1915 the Hassett Road house was occupied by the Hewson family. Philip Hewson is listed here with the trade of pipe-mounter. Henry Smith met and married Philip's sister and eventually they moved into the Hassett Road house. Another member of the Hewson family carved and turned ivory and other materials; some examples are shown in the photograph below. They are, from the left, a one-legged beggar, a shoeblack and a beadle who has lost his pole. They were originally designed as decorations for a wedding cake.

Eight

Time Off: Travel and Entertainment

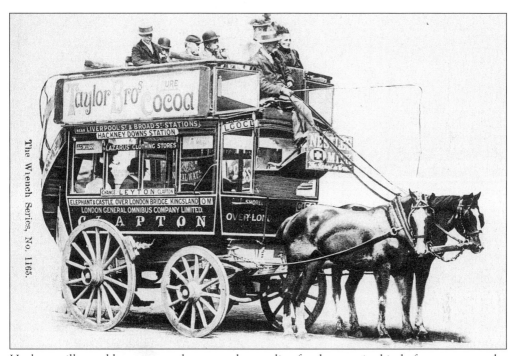

The Wrench Series, No. 1165.

Hackney villas and houses were the smart place to live for the superior kind of commuter to the City of London. Commuters form the Clapton area before the 1870s would have had to use the Great Eastern Railway at Lea Bridge or make for the North London railway station at Hackney – this line also served Dalston, Homerton and Victoria Park. Many business people in 1874 were still travelling into the City by horse-buses which ran every 15 minutes from Stamford Hill and points between there and London. For shorter journeys particularly the horse-trams every 10 minutes were popular. While they remained rural villages, Hackney, Clapton and Shoreditch were great places of resort for pleasure and refreshment for Londoners wanting to get out of the town. Tea and beer gardens provided all kinds of enticing foods, beverages and games. Samuel Pepys' Diary entry for 11 June 1664 reads 'With my wife only to take ayre, it being very warm and pleasant … and thence to Hackney. There light and played at shuffle board; ate ice cream and good cherries and so with good refreshment, home.' The working classes in the nineteenth and twentieth centuries did not fare so well for time off but often made their entertainment at home, as best they could. This led to the universal dream of respectability at the time – owning an upright piano, purchased on easy terms. The less respectable male population – and indeed some of the females – spent large parts of the money they earned on seeking oblivion in drunkenness, a way of combating the drudgery of their daily working situation.

The horse-tram pauses on Clapton Common, 1903.

By the end of Edward VII's reign the electric tram had replaced the horse and the smart vehicles were carrying large numbers of the local population to and from work and leisure activities. This is a scene in Kingsland High Street between no. 71 (left) and no. 84 (right) in 1907. Most of the shoppers are still on foot, however.

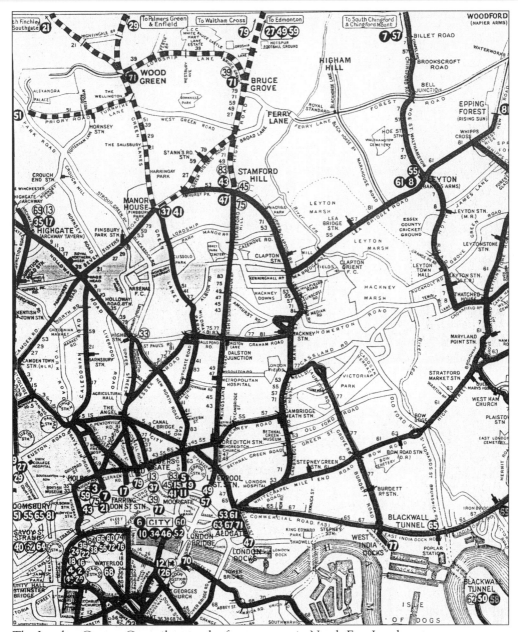

The London County Council network of tram routes in North East London.

In 1903 Rectory Road station boasts a newspaper stand on the platform – justified by the heavy commuter traffic on the North London Railway.

The building of Victoria Park station in the farthest south-east corner of Hackney Borough gave a shot in the arm to industry, business and local workers in the area as well as encouraging more house-building. This handsome building, pictured in 1903 was closed in 1943 due to wartime damage.

Many Hackney commuters travelled into Broad Street station in the City, seen here in a rush hour in 1905.

Going home via Liverpool Street station suburban lines to Hackney Downs, Clapton and Stamford Hill in 1908.

A lazy day in Springfield Park – many busy workers took what little recreation they had here. Mums and children are enjoying the park in 1903.

Waterside fun for children in Victoria Park. The lakes were excavated in 1846, a year after the park was first opened. The process itself must have been interesting to watch.

Going to look at the birds in the aviary at Victoria Park – a popular trip on fine days in Edwardian times.

The staff of the London County Council Hackney Tramways Depot with the athletics trophies they have won. One of the advantages of working for a big employer was the subsidized sports facilities.

Spring Hill on the Lea. A misty day for water activities – but the rowers are making the best of the conditions as they start off from Tyrell's boatyard, home of many clubs in the first two decades of the twentieth century.

Cricket.

A MATCH WILL BE PLAYED,

IN THE

LONDON FIELDS, HACKNEY

On THURSDAY, SEPTEMBER 14th, 1815,

Between eleven Gentlemen of

The Ratcliff Cricket Club,

AND ELEVEN GENTLEMEN OF THE

LONDON CRICKET CLUB,

FOR FIFTY GUINEAS A SIDE.

The Wickets to be pitched at Ten o' Clock.

In 1815 London Fields were being used for cricket matches.

The White Lion at Hackney Wick was a good venue for all kinds of sporting activities in the nineteenth century. The name comes from the emblems of the Knights Templar, the lion and the lamb. The grounds attached to the inn were made into a sporting area known as 'Baum's Running Grounds' and boxing, wrestling and running competitions were put on here in the early nineteenth century.

The Rink Picture Palace, Lower Clapton Road. The cinema was about to rival the variety theatre as a place of entertainment by 1913 but the moving pictures at this stage were silent apart form the piano accompaniment which tried to convey the development of the plot.

53 Malvern Rd
Dalston N.E.
18/8/4

Dear W Ockenden

Just a reminder that Saturday is the day for our bike ride.

Instead of W Cox & I coming over to Ilford, will you meet us at the Eagle at 2.30, & so save time, for the days are getting

A cyclist from Dalston arranges a meeting and a cycling trip with a friend from Ilford.

The ASCENT of Mᴿˢ GRAHAM with the ROYAL VICTORIA BALLOON, Accompanied by Mᴿˢ W.H.Adams and Miss Dean, the only three female Aeronauts that ever ascended alone, from the MERMAID TEA GARENS, HACKNEY on the 9ᵗʰ of August, 1837.

The ascent of Mr Graham's balloon from the Mermaid Tea Gardens, Hackney on 9 August 1837. These events were always a source of great excitement to spectators in the early nineteenth century – they were curious to see if the temperamental equipment (and sometimes balloonists) would be successful in taking off.

107

GRECIAN THEATRE
CITY ROAD.

Proprietor   ...   .   Mr G. CONQUEST

On MONDAY, February 10th, 1873, and Every Evening during the week, to commence with a New and Original Pantomime, written by Mr. GEO. CONQUEST and H. SPRY, entitled

NIX,
THE DEMON DWARF;
OR,
HARLEQUIN, THE SEVEN CHARMED BULLETS, THE FAIRY, THE FIEND, AND WILL-O'-THE-WISP.

Scene 1.—THE KITCHEN RANGE.

Cockchafer, King of the Black Beetles, a bad character,   Mr TUCKER
Zoroaster, (a Demon, proprietor of the bullets) Miss ALICE DENVILLE

Scene 2.—ZOROASTER'S STORE-ROOM.

Nix, the Demon Dwarf (afterwards Fan-Fan)   Mr GEO. CONQUEST
(Will-o'-the-Wisp)   (a light character)   Master GEORGE CONQUEST
Desperado   (by name and nature naughty)   Mr JACKSON

SCENE 3. THE PUBLIC GARDENS.
FLORAL FETE AND ARRIVAL OF THE KING'S COURT.

King Cockaloram (a great king in mind, but small in body) Mr H. LYNN
Count Pomposo (gold stick in waiting, a very stickish stick)   Mr ASH
Bumbleo, the Beadle   (the Beadle—Off with your hats)   Mr BROWN
Bodger, the Cobbler ... (one of nature's noblemen) ...   Mr INCH
Count Kuffie (of striking pugilistic proclivities) Mr JOHN MANNING
Sureaim (Chief Ranger of royal woods and forests) Miss MATTHEWS
Prince Dauntless (loving and beloved of Duxidearie) Miss M. A. VICTOR
The Princess Duxidearie (the King's daughter) Miss L. BEAUMONT
Princess Lankilina (her eldest sister, double her sister's size) Mr DONNE

The Royal Guards, not blackguards, and, therefore, entitled to our regards, by several large bodies of "regular old soldiers."

The Eagle Tavern Pleasure Gardens were originally called the Shepherd and Shepherdess. They were opened in the 1760s off the new route between the City and Islington, the City Road. Thomas Rouse, a builder, created amusements here such as balloon ascents, musical extravaganzas and wrestling.

An example of a playbill for the Grecian Theatre after Mr G. Conquest, a colourful proprietor, had taken over (10 February 1873).

The Eagle later became the Grecian Theatre with a magnificent interior, designed by the architect J.T. Robinson.

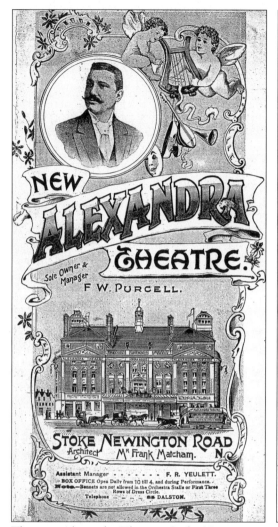

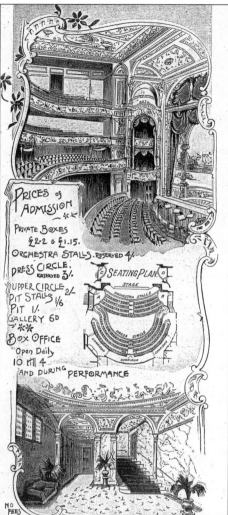

The new Alexandra Theatre, Stoke Newington, was designed by Frank Matcham, one of the most famous Edwardian designers. This delightful programme has illustrations of the exterior and interior as well as the details (opposite) of the performance by Dan Leno, one of the biggest music-hall comedians of the time in a farce called *Gay Piccadilly*. The theatre had opened on 27 December 1897 and was later briefly a cinema. Alexandra Court now stands on the site.

PROGRAMME.

Monday, November 27th, for Six Nights and One Matinee

Mr. MILTON BODE'S COMPANY

Including The Great Drury Lane COMEDIAN, Mr.

DAN LENO

In a New Musical Farce, in Two Acts, entitled

IN GAY PICCADILLY!

By GEORGE R. SIMS and CLARENCE CORRI.

Aubrey Honeybun, } Of Trackem & Trapp, {	... ...	... Mr. DAN LENO
Ebenezer Tinkletop, } Detectives {	... ...	Mr. JOHNNY DANVERS
Lord Dudeville, a Peer	... ...	Mr. CHARLES THORBURN
Guy Brabazon, a Younger Son ...	... ...	Mr. GEORGE SINCLAIR
Montague Miggs, a Company Promoter ...	... ...	...Mr. TIM RYLEY
Bertie Grey }	... ...	... Mr. GEORGE HUDSON
Charlie Vere } Young Men about Town {	... ...	...Mr. EDWARD GRIFFIN
Algv Phipps }	... ...	... Mr. JOHN DANIELS
Attendant at Earl's Court	... ...	... ... Mr. T. HILL
Lady Dudeville, Lord Dudeville's Wife	... ...	Miss FLORENCE DARLEY
Lady Molly Wildgoose, her Daughter	... ...	Miss BEATRICE WILLEY
Mrs. Honeybun, Honeybun's Wife ...	... ...	... Miss EMILY STEVENS
Gladys Ada, a General Servant ...	... ...	Miss ADIE BOYNE
Daisy Delamere, of the Prince's Theatre }	... ...	Miss LILLIE YOUNG
Dolly Flopp, Daisy's Twin Sister }		
Cissy Potts, } Of the {	... ...	Miss E. GRAHAM
Ruby Green, } Prince's Theatre { ...	... ...	Miss P. PEPPIATE

Piccadillians, Theatre Ladies, Flower Girls, Firemen, Brides, Colonial Troopers,
Dairy Maids, Savage South Africans, etc.

ACT 1 - - - **THE CIRCUS, PICCADILLY**

ACT 2 - **"PICTURESQUE ENGLAND," EARL'S COURT**

Solo Dance by Miss RITA BARRINGTON.

Produced by FRANK PARKER. ` Dances by EDOUARD ESPINOSA.

Dresses by STAGG & MANTLE, E. MORRIS & Co., and MORRIS ANGEL & SON.
The Scenery Specially Painted by S. KING ALEXANDER, at the County Theatre, Reading.

General Manager ... ... }	... ...	Mr. STANLEY ROGERS
Assistant Acting Manager... ... }	... ...	Mr. DUDLEY REYNOLDS
Stage Manager ... . } For Mr. MILTON BODE {	... ...	Mr. CHARLES THORBURN
Musical Director ... ... }	... ...	Mr. ARNOLD COOKE
Advance Representative ... ... }	... ...	Mr. W. BUCCLEUCH

The Pianoforte in use at this Theatre supplied by BAGGARLEY, 82, Midmay Park, N.

MATINEE THURSDAY, NOV. 30th, at 2-30.

The WAR in the TRANSVAAL.

By special arrangement with the "Star" and the "Morning Leader" Mr. Purcell is enabled to give the most complete services of War Cables in London, including the services of the "Star" and "Morning Leader's" two War Correspondents, at the front. The Cables will be posted in the Vestibule and Foyer of the Theatre and in the Pit and Upper Circle Saloons.

Monday, December 4th, for One Week
Return Visit of **LA POUPEE**

The Hackney Empire, Hackney's main home for music-hall performances, c. 1908. It had been built at the beginning of the century and all the big stars appeared at this theatre in its heyday. It continues today as a community theatre.

A 1930s programme, from the heyday of the big bands.

ELSIE BOWER and BILLY RUTHERFORD

CLOWNING THRU' THE SHOW

A super-charged human dynamo of volatility and versatility, ELSIE BOWER, merry madcap of Variety, is irrepressible and irresistible.

BILLY RUTHERFORD is a dialect comedian equally at home with the broad "a's" of Lancashire and the dropped "aitches" of the London Cockney.

Isn't she gorgeous? It's ELSIE BOWER

LOW and WEBSTER

" EDUCATE YOURSELF "

NEITHER LOW nor WEBSTER need any lessons in laughmaking ! They exchange quip and crack with the expertness of born arguers. In fact, both of them could more than hold their own in any gab contest. Even though one would like to give the other a punch on the jaw, this is jaw with a " punch " !

MAHONEY BROS.
HUNDRED PER CENT LAUGH JUGGLERS.

KERNS AND CAPON

HE'S GOT WIT AND SHE'S GOT EVERYTHING !

HUMOUR is their strong suit, slick cross-talk is their speciality and their dancing is something to write home about. What more could anyone ask ? We agree with you   just perfect !

LES TERRIANOS

REALLY SENSATIONAL BALANCERS

AMAZING feats of strength in a thrilling performance. They have perfected one trick, claimed to be unique a flying spring-board leap direct on to the hands of the other followed up by a sustained balance.

CAL McCORD

THE " CHORD "IAL CANADIAN

A COWBOY who can exercise his tongue as freely as a rope is this wit from the wide open spaces. He does amazing tricks with a lariat, comments wittily on things generally and radiates a hundred-per-cent personality. Yes ma'am, he sure was wasted on them cows !

The supporting stars and other acts appearing with Roy Fox at the Hackney Empire.

Announcement of the first issue of the *Hackney Gazette* – reading the local paper was many a person's choice for relaxation and entertainment.

The *Gazette's* publication office in former days.

Nine
Shoreditch and Hoxton

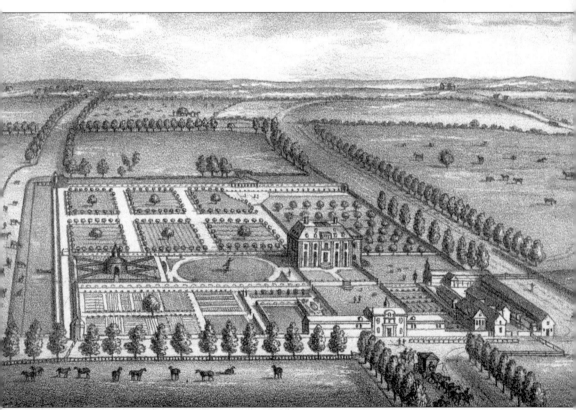

Baumes (or Balmes) House and estate. The house was built by two brothers named Balm in Hoxton around 1540 and what later became Whitmore Road was originally a carriageway to Balmes. It ended up as one of Hoxton's madhouses for which it became famous by 1816.

The Tudor map of the City shows Bishopsgate leading up to Shoreditch and the area of Norton Folgate. Shoreditch's ribbon development contrasts with the activities in the countryside beyond and gardens and summerhouses north of Moorfields. Note the two wells in Bishopsgate.

For hundreds of years archers practised their art beyond Moorfields and towards Islington. They would traverse the fields, firing at marks set up at particular points like this one known as 'Jehu'.

A Finsbury archer's ticket shows the style of dress worn by the fashionable exponent of the sport.

The old St Leonard's church whose tower was well known to the Elizabethan playwrights. A new church was built between 1738 and 1740 by George Dance the Elder.

118

The whipping post and stocks formerly used by Shoreditch Parish as preserved in the churchyard.

This print of stock characters in the early English theatre reminds us of Shoreditch's proud place in the history of theatre in London. As Adcock wrote: 'Shakespear … had left his wife in Stratford to come to London with a troup of travelling players, and, then a young man of about 24, was engaged in some minor capacity at a playhouse named the Theatre, which stood in Shoreditch near where the Standard Theatre was in recent times. It had been built by James Burbage, a Shoreditch carpenter and joiner, who developed into the first of the actor managers and was the father of Richard Burbage, the most famous actor of the Shakespearean era.' The rival theatre in Shoreditch was the Curtain in Holywell Lane built in about 1576. Its actors were called the Lord Chamberlain's Men. It ceased to function about 1625.

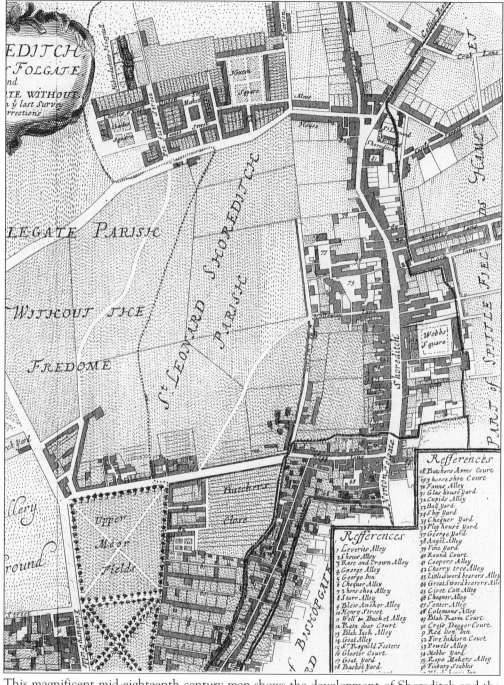

This magnificent mid-eighteenth century map shows the development of Shoreditch and the still open areas by Moorfields and to the north.

The centre of Shoreditch in 1827. The King's Arms inn is on the right.

A vignette of the White Lead Mills and the Rosemary Branch Tavern on the northern edge of Shoreditch Parish, c. 1857. The old tavern is part of the works. A new Rosemary Branch Tavern and tea gardens erected beyond it was a rival to the Eagle Tavern off City Road.

The Britannia Theatre, Hoxton, kept up the tradition of the theatre in Hoxton in the nineteenth century.

The Eastern Counties Railway terminus at Bishopsgate was really in Shoreditch. After it was replaced by Liverpool Street it became a goods station.

Local colour on Haggerston Road in 1910 – homes, shops and a working men's club.

Hoxton Baths, Pitfield Street. The Metropolitan Borough of Shoreditch was very proud of its record in the provision of services and amenities. It issued a series of postcards illustrating them.

Inside Hoxton baths, 1912.

A charity fancy-dress ball at the Town Hall on behalf of disabled soldiers, 5 February 1916.

In the early days of radio BBC broadcasts of music were eagerly listened to in public houses. Here, customers at the Lion and Lamb, Hoxton, 'listen in' to a concert broadcast from Marconi House.

The Salvation Army felt they were driving out the Devil when they acquired the Eagle Tavern and Theatre, off City Road, for their own uses.